Alex Anderson's
babyquilts
WITH LOVE

12 TIMELESS PROJECTS FOR TODAY'S NURSERY

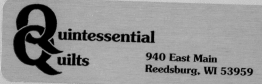

Text © 2006 Alex Anderson

Artwork © 2006 C&T Publishing, Inc.

Publisher: Amy Marson

Editorial Director: Gailen Runge

Acquisitions Editor: Jan Grigsby

Editor: Liz Aneloski

Technical Editors: Teresa Stroin, Wendy Mathson

Copyeditor/Proofreader: Wordfirm, Inc.

Design Director/Cover & Book Designer: Christina Jarumay

Illustrator: John Heisch

Production Assistant: Matt Allen

Photography: Luke Mulks and Diane Pedersen, unless otherwise noted

Published by C&T Publishing, Inc., P.O. Box 1456, Lafayette, CA, 94549

Back cover: *Baby Blessings, Beachcomber Baby, Snowballs and Sherbet*, and *Funky Monkeys*.

Attention Teachers: C&T Publishing, Inc. encourages you to use this book as a text for teaching. Contact us at 800-284-1114 or www.ctpub.com for more information about the C&T Teachers Program.

We take great care to ensure that the information included in our books is accurate and presented in good faith, but no warranty is provided nor results guaranteed. Having no control over the choices of materials or procedures used, neither the author nor C&T Publishing, Inc., shall have any liability to any person or entity with respect to any loss or damage caused directly or indirectly by the information contained in this book. For your convenience, we post an up-to-date listing of corrections on our website (www.ctpub.com). If a correction is not already noted, please contact our customer service department at ctinfo@ctpub.com or at P.O. Box 1456, Lafayette, CA, 94549.

Trademark (™) and registered trademark (®) names are used throughout this book. Rather than use the symbols with every occurrence of a trademark or registered trademark name, we are using the names only in the editorial fashion and to the benefit of the owner, with no intention of infringement.

Library of Congress Cataloging-in-Publication Data

Anderson, Alex

  Alex Anderson's baby quilts with love : 12 timeless projects for today's nursery.

    p. cm.

  ISBN 1-57120-321-4 (paper trade)

  1. Quilting--Patterns. 2. Patchwork--Patterns. 3. Children's quilts.
  I. Title: Baby quilts with love. II. Title.

TT835.A49362 2006

746.46'041--dc22

                                        2005017038

Printed in China

10 9 8 7 6 5 4 3 2 1

Acknowledgments

Thank you to:

C&T Publishing, for believing in me for many years;

Darra Williamson, for keeping me on track despite myself;

Paula Reid and Elizabeth Scott, for lending their incredible quiltmaking talents;

Erica von Voltz, for your attention to detail;

Benartex, Moda, and P&B Textiles, for graciously providing wonderful fabric to play with;

Olfa Products, for great tools to create with; and

Bernina USA, for continued excellence.

Contents

Do you know where my quilt is?

I'm looking for it.

introduction

If you are picking up this book, chances are a baby is arriving soon in the life of someone special to you. It may be a family member or dear friend; perhaps your own life is about to be wonderfully changed by the arrival of a child or grandchild. Can you imagine a more delightful way to welcome a baby into the world than with a snuggly quilt made especially for the anticipated arrival?

I remember well my daughter's famous CC (babou, snuggly, blankie). It was loved and used and basically ended up a colorful wad of cotton with a string long enough to poke in her ear at night. Eventually, the CC was passed along to the cat, who loved it equally well. (To preserve my daughter's dignity, I refuse to say at what age this transfer occurred!) My son also had a blankie, made for him by the mom of my college roommate. He loved that blankie to pieces. I still smile at the memories of both of my children so wrapped in love.

Perhaps you are new to quiltmaking and are taking this blessed life event as an opportunity to try your hand at this beloved craft. The timing couldn't be better (and don't be surprised if you quickly become attached to colorful patches of fabric and snippets of thread!). Perhaps you are an old hand at quilting but are simply looking for a quick and easy quilt to make. Either way, this book is chock-full of darling choices for baby's quilt.

Each quilt is straightforward and easy to construct. All were designed to be made in a timely manner—that is, rather quickly—so the mom will feel relaxed letting baby use and love it with "enthusiasm."

You'll notice the "binkies" (pacifiers) that accompany the instructions for each quilt. These indicate a suggested level of skill for the quiltmaker. One binky signifies a super-easy, beginner-friendly quilt. A three-binky quilt might be better saved for a quilter with a bit of experience under his/her belt. Whichever the case, you'll find none too difficult to tackle if you take your time and follow the step-by-step, generously-illustrated instructions.

One final note: Often quilt books featuring baby quilts are an announcement (spoken or unspoken) of sorts from the author. I must stop any rumors immediately—neither my kids nor I are expecting! (The former would *definitely* be preferable, but only at the appropriate time.) In the meantime, babies are popping up in my life these days, and I have found great joy presenting the moms-to-be with quilts intended for use and love. My wish for you is that a similar opportunity in your life brings you as much happiness and joy.

Is my quilt under here?

. . . Or in here?

Dad, I can't find my quilt, so I'm going to make one myself.

It's time for fabric shopping.

the basics

Choosing and Preparing Your Fabrics

With the exception of specialty fabrics such as Minkee Blankee (see page 54), I recommend that you stick with good-quality, 100% cotton fabric. It looks great in the finished quilt, handles well, and holds up nicely to the "enthusiastic" wear and frequent washing you can expect (and want!) your baby quilt to experience.

Since you know a baby quilt will be washed, I also suggest that you prewash all the fabrics you put into it. Cotton can shrink the first time it is washed, so prewashing eliminates the potential for puckers and distortion in the finished quilt. Prewashing can also remove any excess dyes that might bleed or run when the quilt is washed later. Finally, prewashing removes any chemical residue that might linger from the manufacturing process and irritate the baby's skin.

Rotary Cutting

A rotary cutter is a cutting device that resembles a pizza cutter. It is used with a special self-healing mat and a thick, acrylic ruler, both of which can withstand the cutter's razor-sharp blade. When used properly, a rotary cutter can cut through multiple layers of fabric with ease, speed, and accuracy. It is very sharp and should be used with extreme caution. Practice on some scrap fabric before starting on your project.

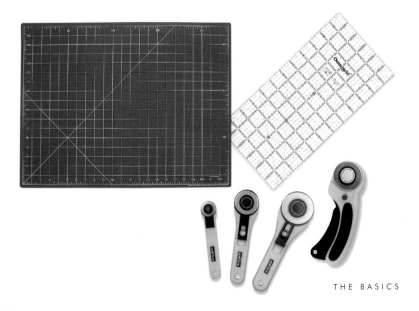

Maybe I spent too much on fabric.

TO CUT A STRIP

Strips can be cut on the crosswise grain, on the lengthwise grain, or on the bias. Before cutting any strips, you must square up the fabric.

1. Fold the fabric selvage to selvage. Fold it again, bringing the first fold up to meet the selvages and lining up the straight of grain as much as possible (4 layers).

2. Position the folded fabric on your cutting mat, keeping the folded edges of the fabric in line with the horizontal lines on the mat.

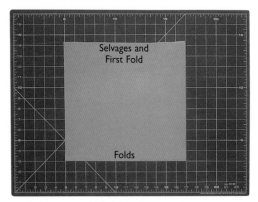

Fold the fabric.

3. Line up the vertical marks on your ruler with the grid on the mat. Place the ruler ½" over the raw edges of the fabric, taking care not to allow your fingers to hang over the side of the ruler where you plan to cut. Rest your pinkie finger on the outside edge of the ruler to keep the ruler from moving.

4. Place the rotary-cutter blade right next to the ruler. Release any safety catch to expose the blade and—cutting away from yourself—make a single pass through the entire length of the fabric to remove the uneven raw edges.

Left-handed   *Right-handed*

Cutting on the Crosswise Grain

The crosswise grain is perpendicular to the selvage. Each project specifies what type of strip to cut, and most are cut on the crosswise grain. The only exceptions are the binding strips for *Petit Fleurs* (cut on the bias) and the sashing and border strips for *Grandma's Favorite* (cut on the lengthwise grain). When a cutting dimension says "by the width of the fabric," cut that strip on the crosswise grain.

1. Complete Steps 1–4 in To Cut a Strip to square up the fabric.

2. Place the ruler on the fabric at the desired width of the cut strip.

3. Make sure the fabric edges and the lines on the ruler are also in alignment with the grid on the mat. Cut the strip.

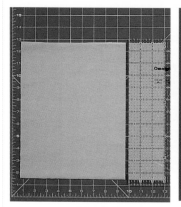 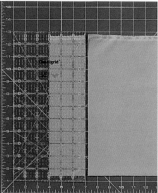

Left-handed   *Right-handed*

Cutting on the Lengthwise Grain

The lengthwise grain runs parallel to the selvage. *Grandma's Favorite* uses this technique for the vertical sashing and borders.

1. Complete Steps 1–4 in To Cut a Strip to square up the fabric.

2. Unfold the fabric once, so you have only 2 layers of fabric to cut through.

3. Keeping the squared and folded edges of the fabric in line with the grid on the mat, place the ruler ½" over the selvage edges of the fabric.

4. Make a single pass with the rotary-cutter blade to remove the selvages.

5. Move the ruler over the fabric to the desired width of the cut strip.

6. Make sure the fabric edges and the lines on the ruler are also in alignment with the grid on the mat. Cut the strip.

> *tip* If you need a strip of fabric wider than your ruler, use the grid lines on your rotary mat to help you cut this wider strip.

TO CUT A SQUARE OR RECTANGLE

1. Cut a strip the width listed in the project instructions and as described in To Cut a Strip on page 6. Square up the ends of the strip as described in Steps 3 and 4 of To Cut a Strip. Be sure the selvages have been removed.

2. Place the strip horizontally on your cutting mat, parallel to one of the grid lines on the mat. You can cut 4 squares or rectangles at a time (4 layers), or open the strip to cut 1 or 2 pieces at a time.

3. Move the ruler over the desired width of the square or rectangle and line up the vertical measurement on the ruler with the trimmed fabric edge. Make sure the fabric edges and the lines on the ruler are also in alignment with the grid on the mat. Cut the square or rectangle.

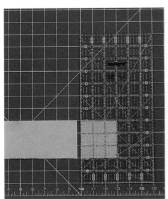

Left-handed

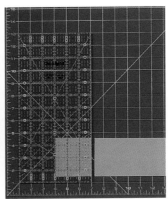

Right-handed

TO CUT A HALF-SQUARE OR A QUARTER-SQUARE TRIANGLE

Although a half-square triangle and a quarter-square triangle may look the same, there is one very important difference. A half-square triangle has two sides—the sides adjacent to the 90° angle—cut on the straight grain. A quarter-square triangle has one side—the long side opposite the 90° angle—cut on the straight grain. Whether you choose to cut a half-square or a quarter-square triangle will depend upon which side of the triangle will fall on the outside edge of the block. It is preferable to have the straight grain fall on the block's outside edge. Both of these triangles begin with a square.

Half-square triangle

Quarter-square triangle

Half-Square Triangle

Cut a square the size listed in the project instructions and as described in To Cut a Square or Rectangle. Position the ruler corner to corner and cut the square in half diagonally to make 2 half-square triangles.

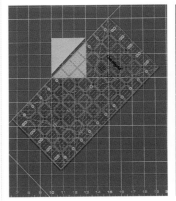

Left-handed

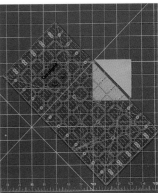

Right-handed

Quarter-Square Triangle

Cut a square the size listed in the project instructions and as described in To Cut a Square or Rectangle on page 7. Position the ruler corner to corner and cut the square in half diagonally in both directions to make 4 quarter-square triangles.

Quarter-square triangles

Pinning

Some quilters pin and some quilters don't. I am a firm believer in pinning, as I have found that the little time it takes to pin can determine the success of the block…and, ultimately, the quilt! Basically, I pin wherever there are seams and intersections that need to line up.

I use quality extra-fine glass-head pins. They are a bit more expensive, but believe me: they are worth the investment. Using poor-quality pins will only cause you headaches.

When aligning seams that are pressed in opposite directions—a common occurrence—place a pin in both sides of the seam, no more than ⅛″ from each side.

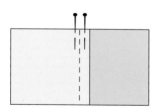

If you have two points that need to match exactly, place the first pin in the wrong side of A, exactly at the intersection, inserting it into the right side of B, exactly at the ¼″ seam allowance. Press the head of the pin firmly into both intersections.

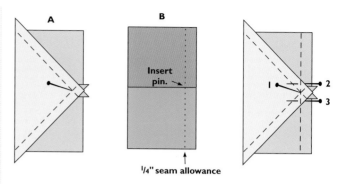

Pin two points to align exactly.

While holding the pin firmly in place, place a second and third pin on each side of the intersection, no more than ⅛″ from the first pin.

As you approach the intersection while sewing the seam, remove the pins right before you stitch over them. Remove pin #1 at the last second, so your sewing machine needle can go into the hole created by the pin. It works!

> ### tip
> In most cases, illustrations show finished units and blocks (no seam allowances). Keep this in mind, especially when making Flying Geese units.
>
>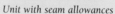
>
> *Unit with seam allowances*   *Finished Unit*

Piecing

Use a ¼″-wide seam allowance unless instructed otherwise. Set the stitch length on your sewing machine just long enough so that your seam ripper slides nicely under the stitch. Backtacking is not necessary if the seam ends will be crossed by other seams.

These are great presents, but where's my sewing machine?

¼"-WIDE SEAM ALLOWANCE

The shapes in this book are all cut with a ¼"-wide seam allowance included, with the exception of *Baby Blessings* (page 53). Some sewing machines come with a foot attachment that measures an exact ¼" seam.

If your machine does not have this feature, you can easily mark your machine to measure this important seam width. Put your clear plastic ruler under the sewing machine needle and drop the presser foot. Manually ease the needle down onto the ruler's ¼" mark. Take a narrow piece of masking tape and mark the ¼" on the throat plate, using the edge of the ruler as your guide.

Use the tape as a seam guide as you sew the pieces together. Sew a few practice seams to test your measurement. If the seam does not measure an exact ¼", remove the tape and try again. "Close enough" will only reward you with yards of frustration.

¼"

Removing Stitches

Occasionally you will want to pick out and restitch a seam. Cut every third thread on one side of the pieced unit, then gently lift the thread off the other side of the fabric.

If you are attempting to remove stitches from two bias edges, consider tossing out the pieces and beginning again rather than ripping out the seam. The chance of stretching the bias edges is almost 100%. If the edges stretch, the shapes won't realign or sew together properly.

Pressing

I usually press seams to one side or the other, but in some cases—for example, if six or more seams are converging in one area—I press the seams open to reduce the bulk. I've included arrows on the illustrations to indicate which way to press the seams.

Press.   Press.

Settings

Setting (or set) refers to the way the blocks are arranged and sewn before the borders are added. The quilts in this book use two different types of sets: the straight set and the diagonal set.

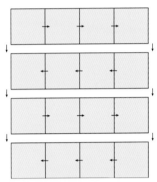

Straight set; sew into vertical or horizontal rows, press, then sew the rows together.

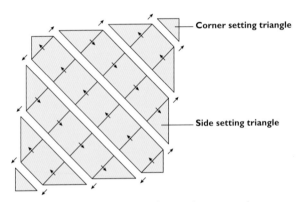

Corner setting triangle

Side setting triangle

Diagonal set; sew into diagonal rows, press, then sew the rows together.

Borders

The quilts in this book feature three different border treatments: butted borders, borders with corner squares, and partial-seam borders.

When fabric strips must be pieced together to achieve the required border length, piece them diagonally. (Refer to the illustrations in Binding, Step 2, on page 13.) Diagonal seams are less noticeable in long strips, such as those used for borders. However, always piece striped fabrics with straight seams, to keep the fabric pattern aligned.

BUTTED BORDERS

Butted borders are the easiest of all borders to stitch, and I have used them for the majority of the quilts.

1. Measure the sewn and pressed quilt top through the center from top to bottom. Trim 2 borders to this measurement, piecing them first, if necessary, to achieve the required length. These will be the side borders.

2. Find the midpoint of the side of the quilt top and the midpoint of a side border strip by folding each in half. With right sides together, pin the border to the quilt top, matching the ends and midpoints, and pinning every 2″ in between, easing or stretching slightly to fit. Sew the border to the quilt top with a ¼″ seam and press as shown. Repeat for the other side border.

3. Measure the quilt top through the center from side to side, including the borders you just added. Cut 2 borders to this measurement, piecing them if necessary. These will be the top and bottom borders.

4. Repeat Step 2 to pin and sew the borders to the top and bottom of the quilt. Press as shown.

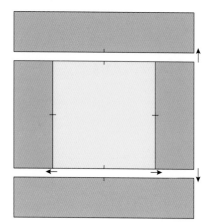

BORDERS WITH CORNER SQUARES

Borders with corner squares are easy to sew, and—here's a little surprise—they can come to your rescue if you run short of border fabric.

1. Measure your quilt top through the center from top to bottom. Cut 2 borders to this measurement, piecing them, if necessary, to achieve the required length. These will be the side borders.

2. Repeat Step 1, this time measuring your quilt from side to side for the top and bottom borders.

3. Stitch the side borders to the quilt as described in Butted Borders, Step 2.

4. Stitch corner squares onto both ends of the top and bottom borders and press as shown.

5. Stitch the borders from Step 4 to the top and bottom of the quilt, carefully matching the corner seams. Press.

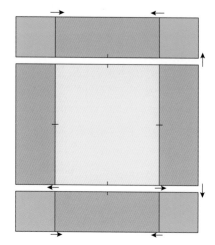

PARTIAL-SEAM BORDERS

Only one quilt in this book (*Little Flyer* on page 40) uses partial-seam borders, but it is a wonderful technique to know.

1. Measure your quilt top from top to bottom through the center. Add the finished width of the border. Cut the side borders to this length.

2. Measure your quilt from side to side through the center. Add the finished width of the border. Cut the top and bottom borders to this length.

3. Find and mark the midpoint on each side of the quilt top as described in Butted Borders, Step 2.

4. From one end of each side border, measure and lightly mark the *length* of the quilt top. Find and crease the midpoint between the end of the strip and the point you've just marked. Repeat for the top and bottom borders, measuring and marking the *width* of the quilt top and creasing to find the midpoint.

5. Place a side border and the right edge of the quilt top right sides together. Match their midpoints, and the bottom right corner of the quilt top with the marked endpoint on the border, and pin. (The border will extend beyond the bottom edge of the quilt.) Align the opposite end of the border strip with the top right corner of the quilt and pin as needed.

6. Stitch the border strip to the quilt top, stopping approximately 3″ from the bottom right corner of the quilt top. Press toward the border.

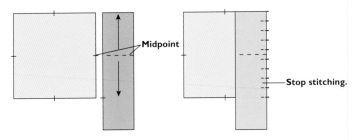

7. Place the top border and the top edge of the quilt top right sides together. Match their midpoints, and the ends of the border with the corners of the quilt. Pin as needed.

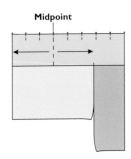

8. Stitch the border to the quilt. Press.

9. Repeat to add the left side border and the bottom border.

10. Complete the first border seam. Press. If necessary, trim and square the corners of the quilt.

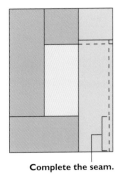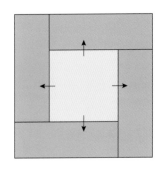

Complete the seam.

Preparing Your Quilt for Quilting

BACKING

If your quilt top is wider than the standard 42″-wide cotton fabric, you will need to piece the backing. Yardages given with the projects take this into account. Regardless of whether or not you must piece the backing, make sure it is at least 2″ larger than the quilt top on all sides (add 4″ to the top's dimensions) to allow for possible shifting during the quilting process. (The same goes for the batting.)

A few other tips for backings:

- If your quilt has a lot of white or very light colors in it, use a light color for the backing. Then the backing won't show through the batting to the front of the quilt.

- It's okay to use more than one fabric for a pieced quilt back. Always prewash and remove the selvage edges before piecing the backing fabric. The selvage is difficult to quilt through, and the resulting seam won't lie flat.

- If you are planning to hand quilt, don't use a sheet or a piece of decorator fabric for the quilt backing. These fabrics have a high thread count and are difficult to quilt. Your fingers will thank you!

tip Soft, cozy flannel makes a wonderful backing for a baby quilt.

BATTING

For hand quilting, I recommend a low-loft, polyester batting. For machine quilting, I recommend that you use 100% cotton batting. Make sure you check the packaging to see if prewashing is required.

Whichever type of batting you select, be sure you cut it at least 2″ larger than the quilt top on all sides.

LAYERING

Depending upon the size of the project, I either work on a tabletop (small quilt) or on my nonloop carpet (large quilt). I use tape or T-pins to secure the backing *wrong* side up, smoothing it from the center to each corner to eliminate wrinkles or "bubbles" and to keep it taut.

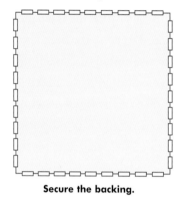

Secure the backing.

Next, carefully unroll the batting and center and smooth it on top of the backing. Finally, center and smooth the pressed quilt top, right side up, over the batting.

Dad, should I machine or hand quilt it?

BASTING

Never skimp on basting! A skimpily or carelessly basted quilt will only cause disaster down the road because the layers may shift, wrinkle, or pucker during the quilting process.

For Hand Quilting

Thread a neutral-colored sewing thread through a large needle, and knot one thread tail. Beginning in the center of the quilt, take large stitches to baste a grid with vertical and horizontal lines about 4″ apart. Don't bother knotting the ending tail of the thread. When it's time to remove the basting, you can just give the knotted end of the thread a tug, and the basting stitches will pull right out.

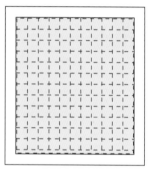

Basting with thread

For Machine Quilting

Rather than using thread, pin baste every 3″ with small (size #1) rustproof safety pins. Pin evenly across the surface of the quilt, avoiding areas where the quilting stitches will be sewn.

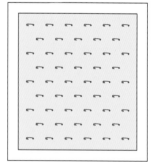

Basting with pins

Quilting

It's just a matter of practice.

I love to hand quilt, but unfortunately I do not always have the time for it. Happily, since these quilts are being made for babies, and will likely end up with lots of loving wear and subsequently lots of laundry time, they lend themselves beautifully to machine quilting.

However, whether you choose to hand or machine quilt, I have three thoughts to share with you:

1. More is better. Never skimp on the amount of quilting on your quilt.

2. Treat the pieced surface as a whole. I rarely quilt ¼″ from the seamlines because it brings the most unsightly part of the quilt (the seams) to the forefront. Therefore, you will often find my quilts quilted with interesting grids or other patterns that ignore the seamlines.

3. Use an equal amount of quilting over the entire surface. If you quilt different areas of the quilt with uneven density, your quilt will not only look odd, but it will sag and not lie flat.

Binding

1. For ⅜″ binding, trim the batting and backing ⅛″ beyond the raw edge of the quilt top.

2. Cut 2⅛″-wide strips from the fabric width, as directed in the project instructions. You will need to piece the strips together to get the desired length. Sew the strips together end to end with diagonal seams, and then press the seams open. This helps prevent a big lump in the binding.

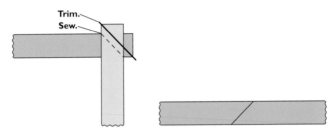

3. Fold and press the binding lengthwise, right sides out.

4. With the raw edges of the quilt top and the binding even, pin the binding to the front of the quilt a few inches from a corner, leaving the first 12″ of the binding unattached. Start sewing, using a ¼″-wide seam allowance from the edge of the quilt top. For pucker-free bindings, use a walking foot attachment (or an even-feed feature if your sewing machine has one). Adjust the needle position to achieve the desired seam allowance.

5. Stop ¼″ from the first corner of the quilt top and backstitch one stitch.

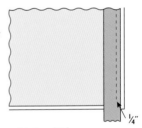

Stitch to ¼″ from corner.

6. Lift the presser foot and needle. Rotate the quilt one-quarter turn. Fold the binding at a right angle so it extends straight above the quilt.

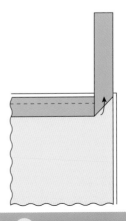

7. Bring the binding strip down, even with the edge of the quilt. Begin sewing again at the folded edge, stopping ¼″ from the next corner and backstitching one stitch.

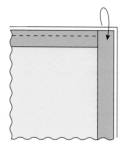

8. Repeat in the same manner at all corners. Stop sewing several inches from where you started stitching the binding to the quilt.

9. Join the ends of the binding by folding the ending binding tail back on itself where it meets the beginning binding tail. From the fold, measure and mark the cut width of your binding strip. Cut the ending binding tail to this measurement. For example, if your binding is cut 2⅛″ wide, measure 2⅛″ from the fold on the ending binding tail and cut the binding tail to this length.

10. Open both tails. Place one tail on top of the other at right angles, right sides together. Mark a diagonal line and stitch on the line. Trim the seam to ¼″. Press open. Refold the binding strip and finish stitching it to the quilt.

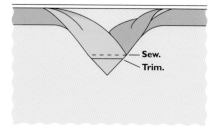

Sew.
Trim.

11. Turn the folded edge of the binding over the raw edge of the quilt and slipstitch the binding to the backing. Form miters at the corners.

tip

For ¼″-wide binding, trim the batting and backing even with the quilt top, machine baste, and stitch the binding to the quilt with ¼″ seam allowance.

CUTTING BIAS STRIPS

Sometimes, particularly when the outside edges of a quilt are curved rather than straight, you'll want to cut the binding strips on the bias, or the diagonal cross-grain of the fabric (see *Petit Fleurs* on page 49). Unlike strips cut on the straight grain (crosswise grain or lengthwise grain), bias strips stretch nicely to accommodate the curved edges.

To cut bias strips, straighten the edge of the fabric as described in To Cut a Strip on page 6. Place the fabric on your cutting mat, aligning the straightened edge of the fabric with a horizontal line on the mat. Position your ruler so the 45° marking is aligned with the straight edge of the fabric. Make a cut.

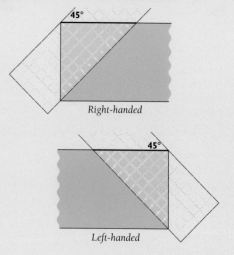

Right-handed

Left-handed

Move the ruler over and align the measurement for the strip width, 2⅛″ in this example, with the trimmed 45° fabric edge. Cut the strip. Continue cutting until you have the number of strips needed to bind your quilt.

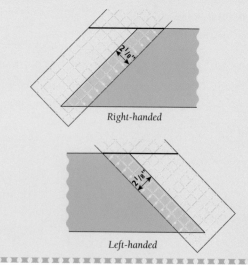

Right-handed

Left-handed

Quilt Label

While I always encourage quiltmakers to label their quilts, I consider a label on a baby quilt an absolute essential. The information you include will be treasured for generations to come. Use a permanent fabric pen on the back (or even on the front) of the quilt, or a beautiful patch designed specifically for the quilt with embroidery or colorful fabric pens. Before sewing the label to the quilt, consider also writing directly on the quilt (where the label will cover) for assurance that the information will not be lost if the label is removed.

Consider including the following information:

- The name of the child
- The child's date and place of birth
- The names of the child's parents
- Your name and the name of the quilter (if different)
- Your relationship to the child
- Where and when the quilt was made
- The special occasion for the quilt (e.g., birth, christening, first birthday)
- Any additional personal sentiments

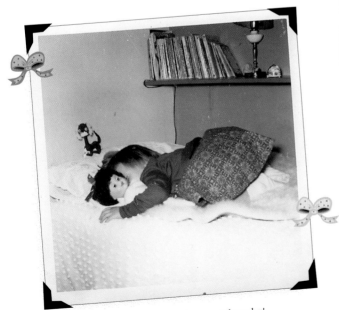

At last, my first quilt to snuggle under!

Caring for the Finished Quilt

If you are giving this quilt to a new mom, you might want to include the following information on the label—copy it and tuck it into a pocket on the back of the quilt, or include it in a note along with the gift. If you are the lucky new mom, this is for you.

Dear Mom,

I am giving you and your precious baby this quilt with the hope that you will enjoy using it…which means that at some time in the future, I know it will need to be cleaned! Here is what I recommend:

1. Fill the basin in your washing machine with cool water, and mix in a mild soap (i.e., one that you would use to launder the baby's clothing and bedding).

2. Place the quilt in the machine and allow it to soak, occasionally swishing the quilt around in the water with gentle hands. *Do not* use the agitate cycle on the washing machine.

3. Allow the quilt to soak for approximately 20 minutes. Advance to the rinse cycle and give the quilt a cool water rinse; then run a gentle spin cycle to remove the excess water.

4. Remove the quilt from the machine and air dry it flat, face down on a large light-colored towel or sheet. If it is a nice day, dry it outdoors. Just be sure it is not in a spot where birds are likely to visit!

Enjoy! Never attach any embellishment that might be pulled free by curious little fingers. If you are in doubt about an item's potential to become a choking hazard, my advice is: Don't use it!

buzzing bumble bees

Buzzing Bumble Bees *Pieced and machine quilted by Alex Anderson, 2004.*

Quilt top size: 40½" × 46½"

Finished block size: 6"

Number of blocks: 30

Skill level: Just simple squares and strips—even a "newbie" can tackle this one!

The adorable bumblebee print determined the color scheme for this easy quilt. I often work this way: I start by choosing a multicolored theme or focus fabric—there are so many adorable novelty prints out there!—and draw my supporting cast of colors from the colors in this key print. If you are intimidated by choosing colors for your quilt, why not give my method a try? Couldn't be simpler!

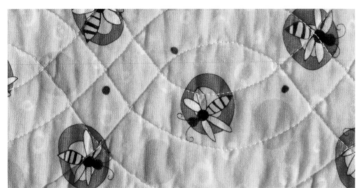

Detail of border (theme) fabric on **Buzzing Bumble Bees.**

Materials

Fabric amounts are based on a 42" fabric width.

Assorted coordinating white-and-black, bright pink, and yellow prints (Fabric A): ½ yard total for blocks

Assorted coordinating black, bright pink, and yellow prints (Fabric B): 1 yard total for blocks

Bright coordinating stripe (Fabric C): ⅓ yard for inner border

Bright yellow bumblebee (or other theme) print (Fabric D): ⅔ yard for outer border

Black-and-white print (Fabric E): ⅜ yard for binding

Backing: 2¾ yards of fabric

Batting: 45" × 51" piece

Cutting

All measurements include a ¼"-wide seam allowance.

Fabric A

▪ Cut a total of 30 squares 3½" × 3½" for the block centers.

Fabric B

▪ Cut a total of 60 rectangles 2" × 3½" in matching pairs for the block bars.
▪ Cut a total of 60 rectangles 2" × 6½" in matching pairs for the block bars.*

Fabric C

▪ Cut 4 strips 2" × the fabric width for the inner border.

Fabric D

▪ Cut 5 strips 4" × the fabric width for the outer border.

Fabric E

▪ Cut 5 strips 2⅛" × the fabric width for the binding.

* *Cut 1 pair to match each pair of 2" × 3½" Fabric B rectangles.*

Making the Blocks

1. Sew a 3½" Fabric A square between 2 matching 2" × 3½" Fabric B rectangles, as shown. Press. Make 30.

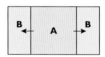

Make 30.

2. Sew matching 2" × 6½" Fabric B rectangles to the top and bottom of each unit from Step 1, as shown. Press. Make 30.

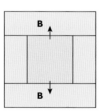

Make 30.

Quilt Assembly

1. Arrange the blocks in 6 horizontal rows of 5 blocks each, turning them as shown in the assembly diagram. Sew the blocks together into rows. Press. Sew the rows together. Press.

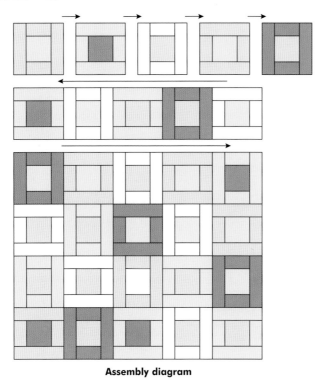

Assembly diagram

2. Refer to Butted Borders on page 10. Measure the quilt top through the center from top to bottom. Trim two 2″-wide Fabric C inner border strips to this measurement. Sew a trimmed border strip to opposite sides of the quilt. Press.

3. Measure the quilt top through the center from side to side, including the borders just added. Trim the remaining 2″-wide inner border strips to this measurement. Sew a trimmed border strip to the top and bottom of the quilt. Press.

4. Repeat Step 2 to trim and sew a 4″-wide Fabric D outer border strip to opposite sides of the quilt. Press.

5. Sew the remaining 4″-wide outer border strips together end to end with diagonal seams. Repeat Step 3 to trim and sew the trimmed strips to the top and bottom of the quilt. Press.

Finishing

Follow the general instructions on pages 11–14 to layer, baste, and quilt your quilt. Sew the 2⅛″-wide Fabric E strips together end to end with diagonal seams and use them to bind the edges.

Snowballs
and sherbet

Snowballs and Sherbet *Pieced by Alex Anderson, 2004. Machine quilted by Paula Reid.*

Quilt top size: 36½" × 41"

Finished block size: 4½"

Number of Snowball blocks: 28

Number of plain blocks: 28

Skill level: Just simple squares and strips—even a "newbie" can tackle this one!

This sweet and simple quilt doesn't use large pieces of any one fabric. It's the perfect choice if you've been hoarding mail-order fabric swatches, been fabric swapping with friends, or have a collection of cherished scraps aching to be used in a special quilt. (Grandma: How about scraps of Mom's childhood clothing?) I used pastels, but bright primary colors or jewel tones are just two alternative color schemes that would work as well.

Materials

Fabric amounts are based on a 42" fabric width.

Assorted yellow, pink, green, blue, and violet pastel prints (Fabric A): 2 yards total for Snowball blocks, plain blocks, and pieced border

Pastel yellow print (Fabric B): ⅜ yard for binding

Backing: 2⅝ yards of fabric

Batting: 41" × 45" piece

Cutting

All measurements include a ¼"-wide seam allowance.

Fabric A
■ Cut a total of 56 squares 5" × 5" for the Snowball and plain blocks.
■ Cut a total of 112 squares 2" × 2" in matching sets of 4 for the Snowball blocks.
■ Cut a total of 64 squares 2¾" × 2¾" for the pieced border.

Fabric B
■ Cut 5 strips 2⅛" × the fabric width for the binding.

Making the Snowball Blocks

1. Draw a line diagonally, corner to corner, on the wrong side of 4 matching 2" Fabric A squares.

2. Place a marked 2" Fabric A square on a corner of a contrasting-colored 5" Fabric A square, right sides together, as shown. Sew directly on the drawn line and trim, leaving a ¼" seam allowance. Press. Repeat with the remaining 3 corners.

3. Repeat Steps 1 and 2 to make 28 blocks.

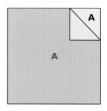

Use contrasting-colored A fabrics.

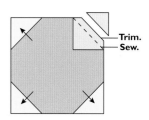

Trim.
Sew.

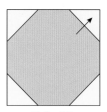

Make 28.

Quilt Assembly

1. Arrange the Snowball blocks and the remaining 5″ Fabric A squares in 8 horizontal rows of 7 blocks/squares each, alternating them as shown in the assembly diagram. Sew the blocks and squares together into rows. Press. Sew the rows together. Press.

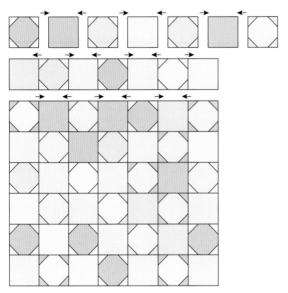

Assembly diagram

2. Sew 16 remaining 2¾″ Fabric A squares together as shown, mixing the colors in a pleasing arrangement. Press. Make 4.

Make 4.

3. Sew 2 units from Step 2 to opposite sides of the quilt. Press. Sew the remaining units to the top and bottom of the quilt. Press.

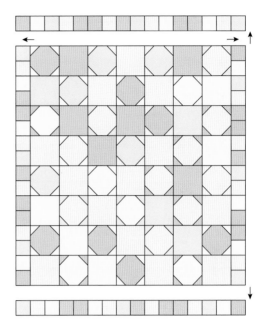

Finishing

Follow the general instructions on pages 11–14 to layer, baste, and quilt your quilt. Sew the 2⅛″-wide Fabric B strips together end to end with diagonal seams and use them to bind the edges.

beachcomber baby

Beachcomber Baby *Pieced and machine quilted by Alex Anderson, 2004.*

Quilt top size: 39½" × 39½"

Skill level: Just simple squares and strips—even a "newbie" can tackle this one!

I loved combining large floral prints in tropical colors with quirky polka dots and stripes in this simple quilt, ideal for the baby born in Southern climates…or who simply loves to splash in the bathtub! You can substitute any large-scale print or fun novelty print for the floral, and use it to determine the rest of the colors for your quilt.

Materials

Fabric amounts are based on a 42" fabric width.

Aqua, pink, and green large-scale tropical print (Fabric A): ⅞ yard for center panel and outer border corner squares

Coordinating stripe (Fabric B): ⅜ yard for inner border

White-and-green polka dot (Fabric C): ⅞ yard for inner border corner squares and Flying Geese units

Medium-scale coordinating tropical print (Fabric D): ⅞ yard for Flying Geese units

Medium-value pink leafy print (Fabric E): ⅜ yard for binding

Backing: 2⅝ yards of fabric

Batting: 44" × 44" piece

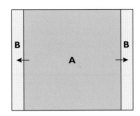 Cutting

All measurements include a ¼"-wide seam allowance.

Fabric A
- Cut 1 square 23½" × 23½" for the center panel.
- Cut 4 squares 6½" × 6½" for the outer border corner squares.

Fabric B
- Cut 4 strips 2½" × 23½" for the inner border.

Fabric C
- Cut 4 squares 2½" × 2½" for the inner border corner squares.
- Cut 6 strips 3½" × the fabric width; then cut 36 rectangles 3½" × 6½" for the Flying Geese units.

Fabric D
- Cut 7 strips 3½" × the fabric width; then cut 72 squares 3½" × 3½" for the Flying Geese units.

Fabric E
- Cut 5 strips 2⅛" × the fabric width for the binding.

 Quilt Assembly

1. Sew a 2½" × 23½" Fabric B inner border strip to opposite sides of the 23½" Fabric A square. Press.

2. Sew a 2½" Fabric C square to the ends of each of the remaining 2½"-wide inner border strips. Make 2.

Make 2.

3. Sew to the top and bottom of the quilt. Press.

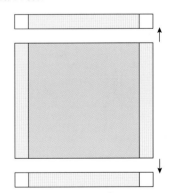

4. Draw a line diagonally, corner to corner, on the wrong side of each 3½" Fabric D square.

5. Align a marked 3½" Fabric D square with one short edge of a 3½" × 6½" Fabric C rectangle, right sides together, as shown.

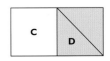

6. Sew directly on the drawn line and trim, leaving a ¼″ seam allowance. Press. Make 36.

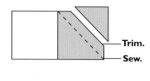

Trim.
Sew.

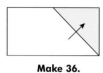

Make 36.

7. Repeat Steps 5 and 6 to sew a 3½″ Fabric D square to the opposite short edge of each of the units from Step 6. Press. Make 36 (see tip page 8).

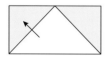

Make 36.

8. Arrange 9 units from Step 7 as shown. Sew the units together. Press. Make 4.

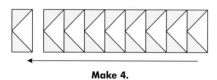

Make 4.

9. Sew a 6½″ Fabric A square to each end of a unit from Step 8. Make 2.

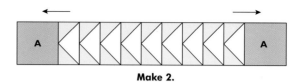

Make 2.

10. Sew a border unit from Step 8 to opposite sides of the quilt. Press. Sew a border unit from Step 9 to the top and bottom of the quilt. Press.

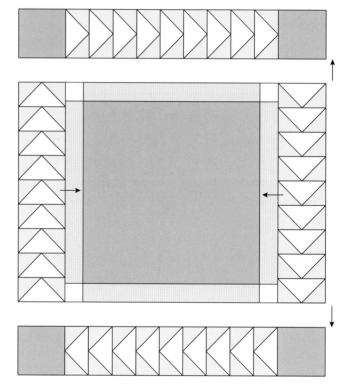

Assembly diagram

Finishing

Follow the general instructions on pages 11–14 to layer, baste, and quilt your quilt. Sew the 2⅛″-wide Fabric E strips together end to end with diagonal seams and use them to bind the edges.

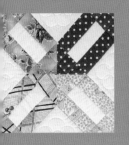

baby Crackers

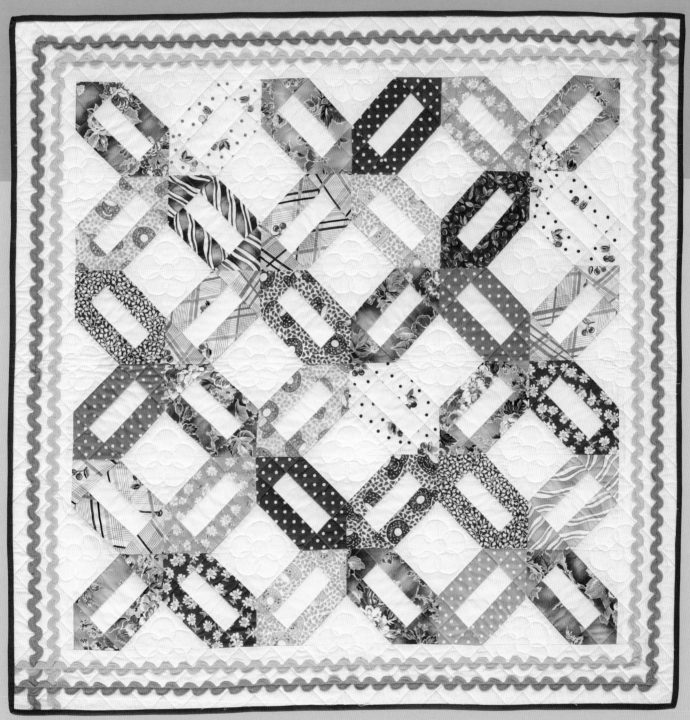

Baby Crackers *Pieced and machine quilted by Alex Anderson, 2004.*

Quilt top size: 39" × 39"

Finished block size: 5¼"

Number of blocks: 36

Skill level: A good choice for a confident beginner.

I paired an off-white solid with a collection of 30s-style pastel reproduction prints and some snazzy rickrack in this cute-as-can-be quilt. It features the traditional Cracker block, a pattern particularly popular in the first half of the twentieth century. The scrappy design would work equally well in any number of color schemes, including crayon brights.

This quilt makes a perfect gift for a baby shower. If you stick with off-white or use another light-colored solid or a light, subtle print for the alternate fabric, guests can sign the blocks with messages for the little newcomer, and Mom will have a wonderful memory of a very special day.

*Detail of border rickrack on **Baby Crackers.***

 Materials

Fabric amounts are based on a 42" fabric width.

Assorted 30s-style pastel prints (Fabric A): 1 yard total for blocks

Off-white solid (Fabric B): 1⅓ yards for blocks and border

Medium blue solid (Fabric C): ⅜ yard for binding

Backing: 2⅝ yards of fabric

Batting: 43" × 43" piece

Rickrack, ½" wide: 4¼ yards each of 2 colors

Thread to match rickrack

 Cutting

All measurements include a ¼"-wide seam allowance.

Fabric A

■ Cut a total of 72 rectangles 1¾" × 4¼" in matching pairs for the blocks.

■ Cut a total of 36 squares 3½" × 3½", then cut each square in half once diagonally to make 2 triangles (72 total) for the blocks.*

Fabric B

■ Cut 4 strips 4" × the fabric width for the border.

■ Cut 4 strips 1¾" × the fabric width, then cut 36 rectangles 1¾" × 4¼" for the blocks.

■ Cut 4 strips 3½" × the fabric width, then cut 36 squares 3½" × 3½". Cut each square in half once diagonally to make 2 triangles (72 total) for the blocks.

Fabric C

■ Cut 5 strips 2⅛" × the fabric width for the binding.

* *Cut 1 square to match each pair of 1¾" × 4¼" (Fabric A) rectangles.*

 Making the Blocks

1. Sew a 1¾" × 4¼" Fabric B rectangle between 2 matching 1¾" × 4¼" Fabric A rectangles, as shown. Press. Make 36.

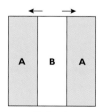

Make 36.

2. Sew matching 3½″ Fabric A triangles to opposite sides of each unit from Step 1, as shown. Press. Make 36.

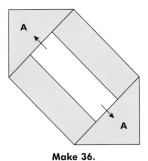

Make 36.

3. Sew 3½″ Fabric B triangles to the remaining sides of each unit from Step 2, as shown. Press. Make 36 (see tip page 8).

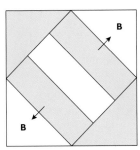

Make 36.

Quilt Assembly

1. Arrange the blocks in 6 horizontal rows of 6 blocks each, turning them as shown in the assembly diagram. Sew the blocks together into rows. Press. Sew the rows together. Press.

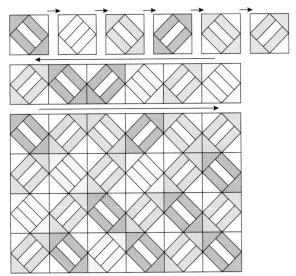

Assembly diagram

2. Refer to Butted Borders on page 10. Measure the quilt top through the center from top to bottom. Trim two 4″-wide Fabric B border strips to this measurement. Sew a trimmed border strip to opposite sides of the quilt. Press the seams toward the border.

3. Measure the quilt top through the center from side to side, including the borders just added. Trim the remaining 4″-wide border strips to this measurement. Sew a trimmed border strip to the top and bottom of the quilt. Press.

Finishing

1. Follow the general instructions on pages 11–14 to layer, baste, and quilt your quilt. Sew the 2⅛″-wide Fabric C strips together end to end with diagonal seams and use them to bind the edges.

2. Cut each piece of rickrack into 2 equal pieces. Refer to the quilt photos on pages 25 and 26 and the diagram. Center 2 pieces of rickrack (one of each color) side by side on adjacent borders of the quilt, as shown. Stitch each piece through the center with matching-colored thread to secure to the quilt. Repeat to stitch rickrack to the remaining sides.

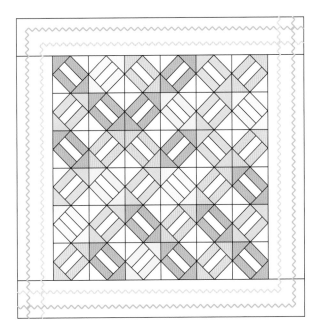

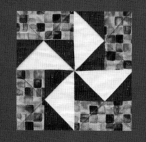

later, alligator!

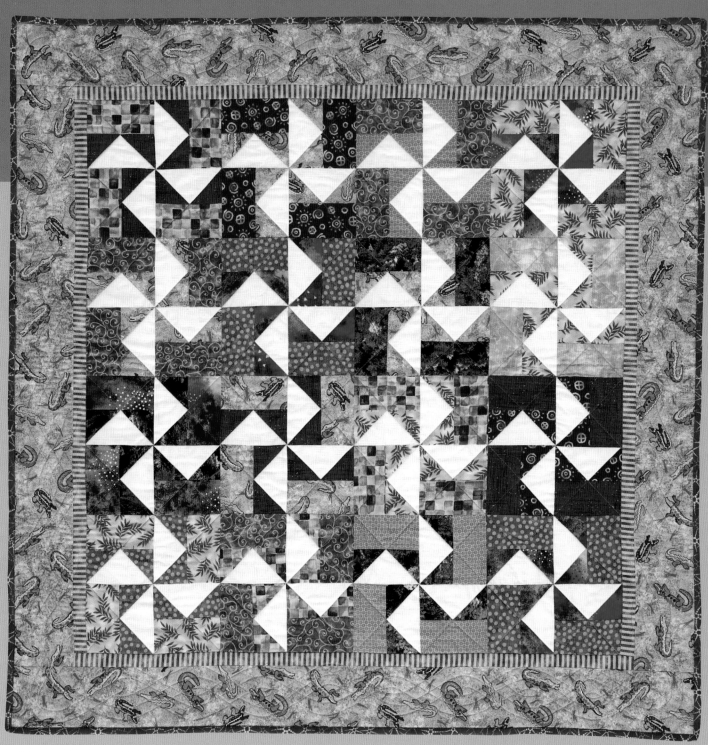

Later, Alligator! *Pieced and machine quilted by Alex Anderson, 2004.*

Quilt top size: 41″ × 41″

Finished block size: 8″

Number of blocks: 16

Skill level: A good choice for a confident beginner.

Here's another quilt featuring a fabulous novelty print. It was easy to choose the rest of the fabrics once I had selected the quirky alligator print. For a change of pace, I used the darker, colorful fabrics for the block backgrounds and used the lightest fabric—a white-on-white print—for the pinwheel motifs. In addition, I used a purple stripe for the inner border. I love using a striped fabric in this spot in my quilts; I feel it adds motion and excitement to the design.

Detail of border (theme) fabric on **Later, Alligator!**

 Materials

Fabric amounts are based on a 42″ fabric width.

Assorted medium-value teal, blue, and purple prints (Fabric A): 1¼ yards total for blocks*

White-on-white print (Fabric B): ⅝ yard for pinwheels

Purple stripe (Fabric C): ¼ yard for inner border

Teal and purple alligator (or other theme) print (Fabric D): ⅔ yard for outer border

Blue print (Fabric E): ⅜ yard for binding

Backing: 2⅝ yards of fabric

Batting: 45″ × 45″ piece

*I used 10 different prints.

 Cutting

All measurements include a ¼″-wide seam allowance.

Fabric A
- Cut a total of 128 squares 2½″ × 2½″ in matching sets of 8 for the block backgrounds.
- Cut a total of 64 rectangles 2½″ × 4½″ in matching sets of 4 for the block backgrounds.

Fabric B
- Cut 64 rectangles 2½″ × 4½″ for the pinwheels.

Fabric C
- Cut 4 strips 1¼″ × the fabric width for the inner border.

Fabric D
- Cut 5 strips 4″ × the fabric width for the outer border.

Fabric E
- Cut 5 strips 2⅛″ × the fabric width for the binding.

 Making the Blocks

1. Draw a line diagonally, corner to corner, on the wrong side of each 2½″ Fabric A square.

2. Align a 2½″ Fabric A square with one short edge of each 2½″ × 4½″ Fabric B rectangle, right sides together, as shown.

3. Sew directly on the drawn line and trim, leaving a ¼″ seam allowance. Press. Make 4 identical units.

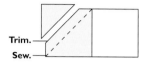

Make 4.

4. Repeat Steps 2 and 3 to sew a matching 2½″ Fabric A square to the opposite short edge of each of the 4 units from Step 3. Press. Make 64 total in matching sets of 4 (see tip page 8).

Make 64 total.

5. Sew a 2½″ × 4½″ Fabric A rectangle in a different print to each unit from Step 4, as shown. Press. Make 64 total in matching sets of 4.

Make 64 total.

6. Arrange 4 matching units from Step 5 as shown. Sew the units together in pairs. Press. Sew the pairs together. Press. Make 16.

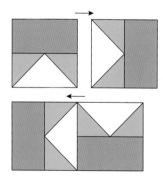

Make 16.

Quilt Assembly

1. Arrange the blocks in 4 horizontal rows of 4 blocks each, as shown in the assembly diagram. Sew the blocks together into rows. Press. Sew the rows together. Press.

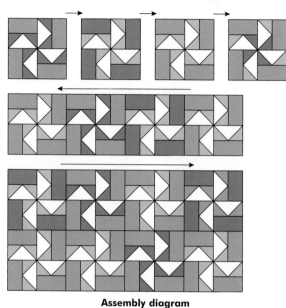

Assembly diagram

2. Refer to Butted Borders on page 10. Measure the quilt top through the center from top to bottom. Trim two 1¼″-wide Fabric C inner border strips to this measurement. Sew a trimmed border strip to opposite sides of the quilt. Press.

3. Measure the quilt top through the center from side to side, including the borders just added. Trim the remaining 1¼″-wide inner border strips to this measurement. Sew a trimmed border strip to the top and bottom of the quilt. Press.

4. Repeat Step 2 to trim and sew a 4″-wide Fabric D outer border strip to opposite sides of the quilt. Press.

5. Sew the remaining 4″-wide outer border strips together end to end with diagonal seams. Repeat Step 3 to trim and sew the trimmed border strips to the top and bottom of the quilt. Press.

Finishing

Follow the general instructions on pages 11–14 to layer, baste, and quilt your quilt. Sew the 2⅛″-wide Fabric E strips together end to end with diagonal seams and use them to bind the edges.

funky monkeys

Funky Monkeys *Pieced and machine quilted by Alex Anderson, 2004.*

Quilt top size: 41″ × 41″

Finished block size: 6″

Number of Monkey Wrench blocks: 9

Number of Snowball blocks: 4

Skill level: A good choice for a confident beginner.

This one was easy! Once I found the terrific "sock monkey" print, the choice of pattern to pair it with was a no-brainer. Alternately called Hole in the Barn Door or Churn Dash, the Monkey Wrench block has a nice center square, perfect for showing off a favorite novelty print. Consider placing a print with a different animal or motif in each block. Not only will you keep your little one warm as he or she grows, but you'll place a source of fun (I Spy) and learning ("This starts with the letter…") in those little hands as well.

Detail of fussy-cut monkey

Detail of backing fabric

 Materials

Fabric amounts are based on a 42″ fabric width.

White-on-white print (Fabric A): ½ yard for Monkey Wrench blocks

Assorted dark brown prints (Fabric B): ⅝ yard total for Monkey Wrench blocks and binding*

Coordinating polka-dot print (Fabric C): ¼ yard for Monkey Wrench blocks

Monkey (or other theme) print (Fabric D): 1 yard for Monkey Wrench blocks and outer border**

Medium red print (Fabric E): ⅝ yard for Snowball blocks, setting triangles, inner border, and corner nine-patches

Medium brown print (Fabric F): ⅞ yard for Snowball blocks, setting triangles, corner squares, and corner nine-patches

Backing: 2⅝ yards of fabric

Batting: 45″ × 45″ piece

*I used 4 different prints.

**You may wish to fussy cut the center squares. Allow extra yardage as necessary.

 Cutting

All measurements include a ¼″-wide seam allowance.

Fabric A

■ Cut 18 squares 2⅞″ × 2⅞″; then cut each square in half once diagonally to make 2 triangles (36 total) for the Monkey Wrench block backgrounds.

Cut 2 strips 2½″ × the fabric width; then cut 36 pieces 1½″ × 2½″ for the Monkey Wrench block backgrounds.

Fabric B

■ Cut a total of 18 squares 2⅞″ × 2⅞″ in matching sets of 2; then cut each square in half once diagonally to make 2 triangles (36 total in matching sets of 4) for the Monkey Wrench blocks.

■ Cut a total of 5 strips 2⅛″ × the fabric width for the binding.

Fabric C

■ Cut 2 strips 2½″ × the fabric width; then cut 36 pieces 1½″ × 2½″ for the Monkey Wrench blocks.

Fabric D

■ Cut 4 strips 6½″ × the fabric width for the outer border.

■ Cut 9 squares 2½″ × 2½″ for the Monkey Wrench center squares.

Fabric E

■ Cut 3 strips 2½″ × the fabric width; then cut 44 squares 2½″ × 2½″ for the Snowball blocks, setting triangles, and corner nine-patches.

■ Cut 4 strips 2″ × the fabric width for the inner border.

Fabric F

■ Cut 4 squares 6½″ × 6½″ for the Snowball blocks.

■ Cut 2 squares 9¾″ × 9¾″; then cut each square in half twice diagonally to make 4 triangles (8 total) for the side setting triangles.

■ Cut 2 squares 5⅛″ × 5⅛″; then cut each square in half once diagonally to make 2 triangles (4 total) for the corner setting triangles.

■ Cut 4 squares 2″ × 2″ for the corner squares.

■ Cut 16 squares 2½″ × 2½″ for the corner nine-patches.

Making the Monkey Wrench Blocks

1. Sew a Fabric A triangle right sides together with a Fabric B triangle, as shown. Press. Make 36.

Make 36.

2. Sew a 1½″ × 2½″ Fabric A piece to a 1½″ × 2½″ Fabric C piece. Press. Make 36.

Make 36.

3. Arrange 4 matching units from Step 1, 4 units from Step 2, and a 2½″ Fabric D square as shown. Sew the units and squares into rows. Press. Sew the rows together. Press. Make 9.

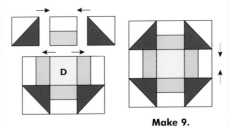

Make 9.

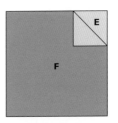

Making the Snowball Blocks

1. Draw a line diagonally, corner to corner, on the wrong side of each 2½″ Fabric E square. Set 8 squares aside for the setting triangles.

2. Place a marked 2½″ Fabric E square on a corner of a 6½″ Fabric F square, right sides together, as shown. Sew directly on the drawn lines and trim, leaving a ¼″ seam allowance. Press. Repeat for the remaining 3 corners.

3. Repeat Step 2 to make 4 blocks.

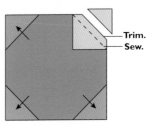

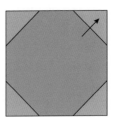

Make 4.

Making the Side Setting Triangles

1. Place a remaining marked 2½″ Fabric E square on the right-angle corner of each large Fabric F side setting triangle (cut from a 9¾″ square), right sides together, as shown.

2. Sew directly on the drawn lines and trim, leaving a ¼″ seam allowance. Press.

3. Repeat Steps 1 and 2 to make 8 side setting triangles.

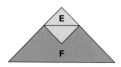

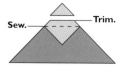

Make 8.

Quilt Assembly

1. Arrange the Monkey Wrench and Snowball blocks on point, alternating them as shown in the assembly diagram. Finish with the pieced side setting triangles from Step 3 and the smaller corner setting triangles (cut from a 5⅛″ square).

2. Stitch the blocks, pieced side triangles, and corner triangles in diagonal rows. Press. Sew the rows together. Press.

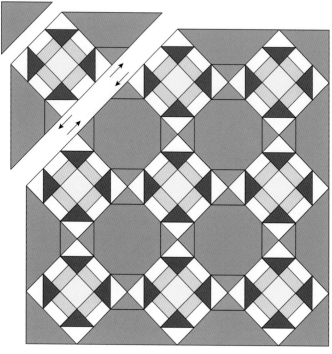

Assembly diagram

3. Refer to Borders with Corner Squares on page 10. Measure the quilt top through the center from top to bottom. Trim each 2″-wide Fabric E inner border strip to this measurement. Sew a trimmed border strip to opposite sides of the quilt. Press toward the border strip.

4. Sew a 2″ Fabric F square to each end of each remaining 2″-wide inner border strip. Make 2. Sew these pieced border strips to the top and bottom of the quilt. Press.

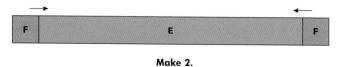

Make 2.

5. Arrange five 2½˝ Fabric E squares and four 2½˝ Fabric F squares as shown. Sew the squares into rows. Press. Sew the rows together. Press. Make 4.

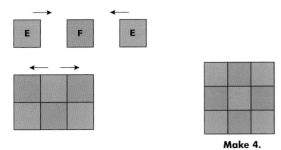

Make 4.

6. Measure the quilt top through the center from top to bottom, including the inner borders already added. Trim each 6½˝-wide Fabric D outer border strip to this measurement. Sew a trimmed border strip to opposite sides of the quilt. Press.

7. Sew a nine-patch unit from Step 5 to each end of each remaining 6½˝-wide outer border strip. Make 2. Sew these pieced border strips to the top and bottom of the quilt. Press.

Make 2.

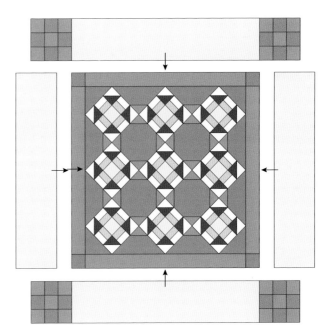

Border assembley diagram

✦ Finishing

Follow the general instructions on pages 11–14 to layer, baste, and quilt your quilt. Sew the 2⅛˝-wide Fabric B strips together end to end with diagonal seams and use them to bind the edges. For this quilt, I used an assortment of the Fabric B prints for the binding.

tree of life

Tree of Life *Pieced by Alex Anderson, 2004. Machine quilted by Paula Reid.*

Quilt top size: 37½″ × 37½″

Finished block size: 25″

Number of blocks: 1

Skill level: A good choice for a confident beginner.

The single large center block in this softly colored quilt offers lots of opportunities for personal touches, not just for baby but for the entire family. Add family names and dates to the "triangle" leaves with embroidery or permanent marking pens, turning the quilt into a true family tree. Trace the hands of parents and siblings for quilting in the large open areas; you can add the baby's handprints and/or footprints after the big day arrives. What a wonderful addition to baby's new world!

Quilted handprints

 Materials

Fabric amounts are based on a 42″ fabric width.

Assorted light- and medium-value sage green prints (Fabric A): 1 yard total for block and binding*

White-on-white print (Fabric B): 1⅛ yards for block background and inner border

Large-scale pink and sage green rose (or other theme) print (Fabric C): ⅔ yard for outer border

Backing: 2½ yards of fabric

Batting: 42″ × 42″ piece

* I used 6 different prints.

Cutting

All measurements include a ¼″-wide seam allowance.

Fabric A

■ Cut a total of 10 squares 5⅞″ × 5⅞″ for the blocks; then cut each square in half once diagonally to make 2 triangles (20 total) for the block. You will have 1 triangle left over.

■ Cut 1 square 6½″ × 6½″ for the block.

■ Cut 1 rectangle 4¾″ × 14½″ for the block.

■ Cut 4 strips 2⅛″ × the fabric width for the binding.

Fabric B

■ Cut 8 squares 5⅞″ × 5⅞″ for the block background; then cut each square in half once diagonally to make 2 triangles (16 total) for the block. You will have 1 triangle left over.

■ Cut 1 square 18¼″ × 18¼″; then cut the square in half twice diagonally to make 4 triangles for the block. You will have 2 triangles left over.

■ Cut 4 strips 2½″ × the fabric width for the inner border.

Fabric C

■ Cut 4 strips 4½″ × the fabric width for the outer border.

Making the Block

1. Sew a Fabric A triangle right sides together with a small Fabric B triangle (cut from a 5⅞″ square), as shown. Press. Make 15.

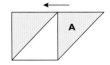

Make 15.

2. Arrange 5 units from Step 1 as shown. Sew the units together. Press.

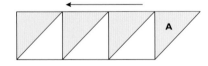

3. Arrange 4 units from Step 1 and a Fabric A triangle as shown. Sew the units and triangle together. Press. Repeat using 3 units and a triangle; 2 units and a triangle; and 1 unit and a triangle. Press.

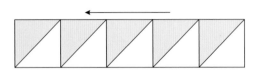

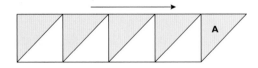

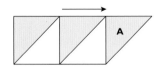

4. Arrange the rows from Steps 2 and 3 as shown. Sew the rows together. Press.

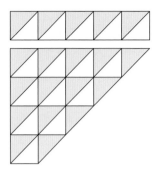

5. Measure and mark the center of one of the short sides of the 4¾″ × 14½″ Fabric A rectangle. Place the 45° line of your quilter's ruler along the top edge of the Fabric A rectangle. Trim twice to your center mark at a 90° angle, as shown.

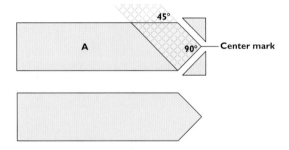

6. Sew a large Fabric B triangle (cut from an 18¼″ square) to opposite sides of the trimmed rectangle from Step 5, as shown. Press.

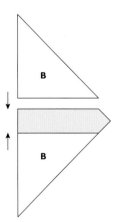

7. Draw a line diagonally, corner to corner, on the wrong side of the 6½˝ Fabric A square. Align the square with the 90° corner of the unit from Step 6, right sides together, as shown. Sew directly on the drawn line and trim, leaving a ¼˝ seam allowance. Press.

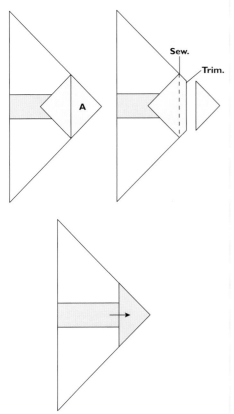

8. Sew the unit from Step 4 to the unit from Step 7, as shown. Press.

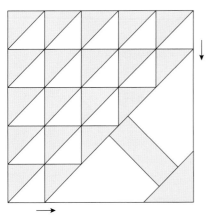

Quilt Assembly

1. Refer to Butted Borders on page 10. Measure the quilt top through the center from top to bottom. Trim two 2½˝-wide Fabric B inner border strips to this measurement. Sew a trimmed border strip to opposite sides of the quilt. Press.

2. Measure the quilt top through the center from side to side, including the borders just added. Trim the remaining 2½˝-wide inner border strips to this measurement. Sew a trimmed border strip to the top and bottom of the quilt. Press.

3. Repeat Steps 1 and 2 to trim and sew the 4½˝-wide Fabric C outer border strips to the sides, top, and bottom of the quilt. Press.

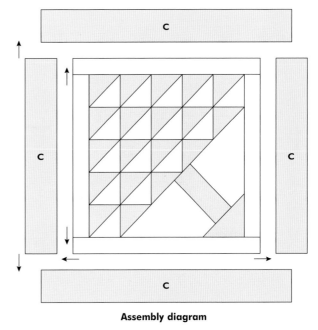

Assembly diagram

Finishing

Follow the general instructions on pages 11–14 to layer, baste, and quilt your quilt. Sew the 2⅛˝-wide Fabric A strips together end to end with diagonal seams and use them to bind the edges. For this quilt, I used an assortment of the Fabric A prints for the binding.

little flyer

Little Flyer *Pieced by Alex Anderson, 2004. Machine quilted by Paula Reid.*

Quilt top size: 41½″ × 41½″

Skill level: A good choice for a confident beginner.

Sometimes a quilt has a mind of its own, and *Little Flyer* is a perfect example. I originally came up with the design and the color scheme with the intention of making a "cowboy" quilt. I even found—I thought—the perfect cowboy-themed border fabric. When I got the center of the quilt pieced, however, I discovered that the border print I had chosen didn't work at all! My search for a replacement turned up this darling airplane print. *Little Cowpoke* became *Little Flyer*…and you'd never know if I hadn't told you. The lesson? Don't feel confined by your original choices. Sometimes Plan B works best after all!

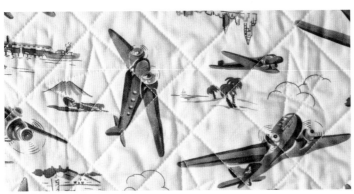

Detail of border fabric on **Little Flyer**

 Materials

Fabric amounts are based on a 42″ fabric width.

Assorted white-on-white, cream, and gray prints (Fabric A): ⅜ yard total for blocks

Assorted blue prints (Fabric B): ⅝ yard total for sashing

Gray plaid (Fabric C): ¼ yard for blocks

Assorted red prints (Fabric D): ¼ yard total for corner squares

Black-and-white plaid (Fabric E): ¼ yard for setting triangles

Black-and-white circle print (Fabric F): ¼ yard for setting triangles

Red plaid (Fabric G): ¼ yard for inner border

White, red, and blue airplane (or other theme) print (Fabric H): ⅝ yard for outer border

Medium-value blue print (Fabric I): ⅜ yard for binding

Backing: 2⅝ yards of fabric

Batting: 45″ × 45″ piece

 Cutting

All measurements include a ¼″-wide seam allowance.

Fabric A
- Cut a total of 29 squares 3¼″ × 3¼″ for the blocks.

Fabric B
- Cut a total of 100 rectangles 1⅞″ × 3¼″ for the sashing.

Fabric C
- Cut a total of 12 squares 3¼″ × 3¼″ for the blocks.

Fabric D
- Cut a total of 60 squares 1⅞″ × 1⅞″ for the corner squares.

Fabric E
- Cut 2 squares 7⅛″ × 7⅛″; then cut each square twice diagonally to make 4 triangles (8 total) for the side setting triangles.
- Cut 1 square 4¾″ × 4¾″; then cut the square once diagonally to make 2 triangles for the corner setting triangles.

Fabric F
- Cut 2 squares 7⅛″ × 7⅛″; then cut each square twice diagonally to make 4 triangles (8 total) for the side setting triangles.
- Cut 1 square 4¾″ × 4¾″; then cut the square once diagonally to make 2 triangles for the corner setting triangles.

Fabric G
- Cut 4 strips 1½″ × the fabric width for the inner border.

Fabric H
- Cut 4 strips 4½″ × the fabric width for the outer border.

Fabric I
- Cut 5 strips 2⅛″ × the fabric width for the binding.

Quilt Assembly

1. Sew one 3¼″ Fabric A square between two 1⅞″ × 3¼″ Fabric B rectangles, as shown. Press. Make 2.

Make 2.

2. Arrange and sew two 3¼″ Fabric A squares, one 3¼″ Fabric C square, and four 1⅞″ × 3¼″ Fabric B rectangles, alternating them as shown. Press. Make 2.

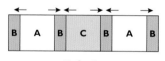

Make 2.

3. Arrange and sew three 3¼″ Fabric A squares, two 3¼″ Fabric C squares, and six 1⅞″ × 3¼″ Fabric B rectangles, alternating them as shown. Press. Make 2.

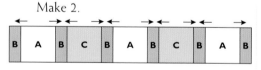

Make 2.

4. Arrange and sew five 3¼″ Fabric A squares, two 3¼″ Fabric C squares, and eight 1⅞″ × 3¼″ Fabric B rectangles, alternating them as shown. Press. Make 2.

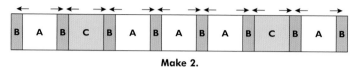

Make 2.

5. Arrange and sew seven 3¼″ Fabric A squares, two 3¼″ Fabric C squares, and ten 1⅞″ × 3¼″ Fabric B rectangles, alternating them as shown. Press. Make 1.

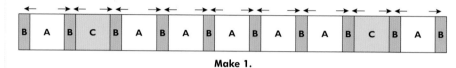

Make 1.

6. Sew one 1⅞″ × 3¼″ Fabric B rectangle between two 1⅞″ Fabric D squares, as shown. Press. Make 2. Sew one of these units to a unit from Step 1. Press. Make 2.

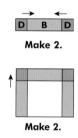

Make 2.

Make 2.

7. Arrange and sew three 1⅞″ × 3¼″ Fabric B rectangles and four 1⅞″ Fabric D squares, alternating them as shown. Press. Make 2. Sew one of these units to a unit from Step 2. Press. Make 2.

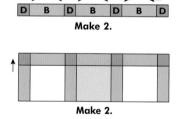

Make 2.

Make 2.

8. Arrange and sew five 1⅞″ × 3¼″ Fabric B rectangles and six 1⅞″ Fabric D squares, alternating them as shown. Press. Make 2. Sew one of these units to a unit from Step 3. Press. Make 2.

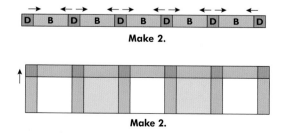

Make 2.

Make 2.

9. Arrange and sew seven 1⅞″ × 3¼″ Fabric B rectangles and eight 1⅞″ Fabric D squares, alternating them as shown. Press. Make 2. Sew one of these units to a unit from Step 4. Press. Make 2.

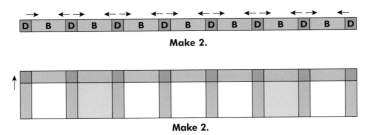

Make 2.

Make 2.

10. Arrange and sew nine 1⅞″ × 3¼″ Fabric B rectangles and ten 1⅞″ Fabric D squares, alternating them as shown. Press. Make 2. Sew one of these units to opposite sides of the unit from Step 5. Press. Make 1.

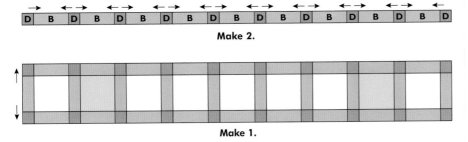

Make 2.

Make 1.

11. Arrange the units from Steps 6–10, the Fabric E side and corner setting triangles, and the Fabric F side and corner setting triangles in diagonal rows, as shown in the assembly diagram.

12. Sew the Fabric E and/or F side setting triangles to each row to complete the row. Press. Sew the rows together. Press. Add the Fabric E and F corner setting triangles. Press.

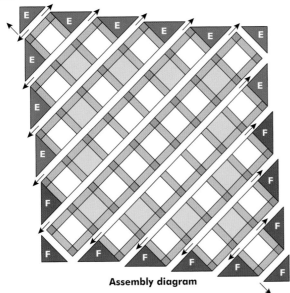

Assembly diagram

 Borders

1. Refer to Butted Borders on page 10. Measure the quilt top through the center from top to bottom. Trim two 1½″-wide Fabric G inner border strips to this measurement. Sew a trimmed border strip to opposite sides of the quilt. Press.

2. Measure the quilt top through the center from side to side, including the borders just added. Trim the remaining 1½″-wide inner border strips to this measurement. Sew a trimmed border strip to the top and bottom of the quilt. Press.

3. Refer to Partial-Seam Borders on page 10 to trim and sew the 4½″-wide Fabric H outer borders to the quilt top. Press.

 Finishing

Follow the general instructions on pages 11–14 to layer, baste, and quilt your quilt. Sew the 2⅛″-wide Fabric I strips together end to end with diagonal seams and use them to bind the edges.

baby baskets

Baby Baskets *Pieced and machine quilted by Elizabeth Scott, 2004.*

Quilt top size: 40½″ × 40½″

Finished block size: 6″

Number of Basket blocks: 13

Skill level: A bit more challenging, but you can do it!

With its delicate pattern and fresh red, pink, and white color scheme, this sweet quilt just seems to whisper—dare I say it?—"little girl." However, with a few simple modifications to the fabric choices—brown or yellow baskets, bright multicolored triangle "fruit" or "flowers"—this quilt would be at home in *any* nursery. Elizabeth's choice of a cherry-striped print adds personality to the binding. For even more "action," try cutting striped binding on the bias. You'll need a bit more fabric, but the results will be fantastic.

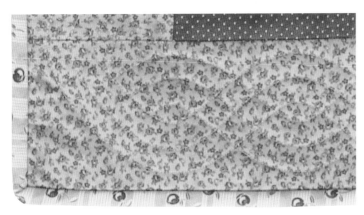

*Detail of striped binding on **Baby Baskets***

 Materials

Fabric amounts are based on a 42″ fabric width.

White-on-white print (Fabric A): ½ yard for blocks

Assorted pink prints (Fabric B): 1 yard total for blocks and plain blocks*

Red pin dot (Fabric C): ⅝ yard for blocks and inner border

Medium-value pink print (Fabric D): ⅔ yard for outer border**

Pink-and-white cherry stripe (Fabric E): ⅜ yard for binding***

Backing: 2⅝ yards of fabric

Batting: 44″ × 44″ piece

* *Elizabeth used 5 different pink prints.*

** *Elizabeth used one of the same medium-value pink prints she used for the blocks.*

*** *You'll need ⅔ yard if you prefer to cut your striped binding on the bias. See page 14.*

 Cutting

All measurements include a ¼″-wide seam allowance.

Fabric A

- Cut 3 strips 2″ × the fabric width; then cut 31 squares 2″ × 2″ and 20 rectangles 2″ × 3½″ for the blocks.
- Cut 3 squares 3⅞″ × 3⅞″; then cut each square in half once diagonally to make 2 triangles (6 total) for the blocks. You will have 1 triangle left over.

Fabric B

- Cut a total of 18 squares 2″ × 2″ in matching sets of 2 for the block centers.
- Cut a total of 8 squares 2″ × 2″ for the block backgrounds.*
- Cut a total of 32 rectangles 2″ × 3½″ in matching sets of 4 for the block backgrounds.*
- Cut a total of 8 squares 3⅞″ × 3⅞″; then cut each square in half once diagonally to make 2 triangles (16 total) for the block backgrounds. You will use 1 triangle from each pair.*
- Cut 12 squares 6½″ × 6½″ for the plain squares.

* *For each block's background, cut one 2″ square, four 2″ × 3½″ rectangles, and one 3⅞″ square from the same fabric. If you are duplicating some of the background fabrics, you may be able to cut fewer 3⅞″ squares and use both triangles from each square.*

Fabric C

■ Cut 3 strips 2″ × the fabric width; then cut 60 squares 2″ × 2″ for the blocks.

■ Cut 1 strip 2⅜″ × the fabric width; then cut 13 squares. Cut each square in half once diagonally to make 2 triangles (26 total) for the blocks.

■ Cut 4 strips 1½″ × the fabric width for the inner border.

Fabric D

■ Cut 4 strips 4½″ × the fabric width for the outer border.

Fabric E

■ Cut 5 strips 2⅛″ × the fabric width for the binding.

(If you are cutting strips on the bias, cut 2⅛″-wide bias strips to total 180″.)

Making the Blocks

1. Arrange two 2″ matching Fabric A squares and two 2″ matching Fabric B squares as shown. Sew the squares together. Press. Sew the rows together. Press. Make 9.

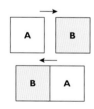

Make 9.

2. Repeat Step 1 using two 2″ matching Fabric A squares and two 2″ Fabric C squares. Press. Make 4.

Make 4.

3. Draw a line diagonally, corner to corner, on the wrong side of each remaining 2″ Fabric C square.

4. Align a marked 2″ Fabric C square with one short edge of a 2″ × 3½″ Fabric A rectangle or 2″ × 3½″ Fabric B rectangle, right sides together, as shown. Make 10 units with Fabric A. Make 16 units in 8 matching sets of 2 with Fabric B.

Make 10.

Make 16.

5. Sew directly on the drawn line and trim, leaving a ¼″ seam allowance. Press.

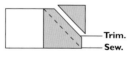

6. Repeat Steps 4 and 5 to sew a matching Fabric C square to the opposite side of each unit. Press. Make 10 units with Fabric A. Make 16 units in 8 matching sets of 2 with Fabric B (see tip, page 8).

Make 10.

Make 16.

7. Sew one unit from Step 6 to one side of a matching unit from Step 1 or 2, as shown. Press. Make 13 total.

Make 4.

Make 5.

Make 4.

8. Sew a matching (Fabric A or Fabric B) 2″ square to each remaining unit from Step 6, as shown. Press. Make 13 total.

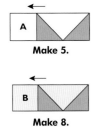

Make 5.

Make 8.

9. Sew each unit from Step 8 to a matching unit from Step 7, as shown. Press. Make 13 total.

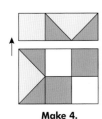

Make 4.

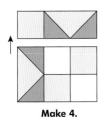

Make 5.

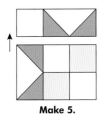

Make 4.

10. Sew a Fabric C triangle to each remaining 2″ × 3½″ Fabric A rectangle or 2″ × 3½″ Fabric B rectangle, as shown. Press. Make 26 total in matching sets of 2 mirror images.

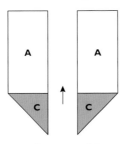

Make 5 sets of 2.

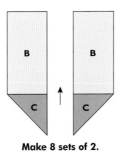

Make 8 sets of 2.

11. Sew 2 matching units from Step 10 to a matching unit from Step 9, as shown. Press. Make 13 total.

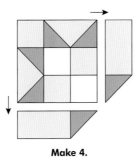

Make 4.

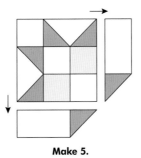

Make 5.

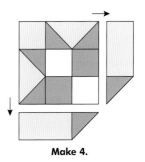

Make 4.

12. Sew a matching Fabric A or Fabric B triangle to each unit from Step 11. Press. Make 13 total.

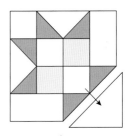

Make 4.

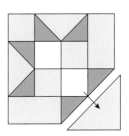

Make 5.

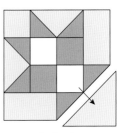

Make 4.

Quilt Assembly

1. Arrange the Basket blocks and the 6½″ Fabric B squares in 5 horizontal rows of 5 blocks each, alternating them as shown in the assembly diagram. Sew the blocks and squares together into rows. Press. Sew the rows together. Press.

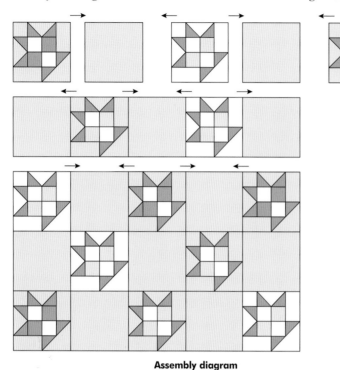

Assembly diagram

2. Refer to Butted Borders on page 10. Measure the quilt top through the center from top to bottom. Trim two 1½″-wide Fabric C inner border strips to this measurement. Sew a trimmed border strip to opposite sides of the quilt. Press.

3. Measure the quilt top through the center from side to side, including the borders just added. Trim the remaining 1½″-wide inner border strips to this measurement. Sew a trimmed border strip to the top and bottom of the quilt. Press.

4. Repeat Steps 2 and 3 to trim and sew the 4½″-wide Fabric D outer border strips to the top, bottom, and sides of the quilt. Press.

Finishing

Follow the general instructions on pages 11–14 to layer, baste, and quilt your quilt. Sew the assorted 2⅛″-wide Fabric E strips together end to end with diagonal seams and use them to bind the edges.

> *tip*
> Elizabeth quilted *Baby Baskets* with pink quilting thread for an extra-rosy glow.

petit fleurs

Petit Fleurs *Pieced and machine quilted by Alex Anderson, 2004.*

Quilt top size: 37½″ × 41½″

Skill level: A bit more challenging, but you can do it!

(This becomes a  one-binky quilt if you eliminate the scalloped edge and substitute a traditional straight-edged border. Refer to Binding, pages 13–14.)

Here's a quilt perfect for the mom (and baby!) who prefers something a little different in nursery décor. I chose a sophisticated toile print for this (almost) wholecloth quilt, but you could substitute any one of the fabulous decorator-style, large-scale floral cotton prints available today. A scalloped edge adds a touch of elegance and interest to this otherwise simple design.

 Materials

Fabric amounts are based on a 42″ fabric width.

Black-and-white toile print (Fabric A): 1¾ yards for center panel and outer border

Black-and-white subtle plaid (Fabric B): ¼ yard for inner border

Black solid (Fabric C): ¾ yard for binding

Backing: 2½ yards of fabric

Batting: 42″ × 46″ piece

 Cutting

All measurements include a ¼″-wide seam allowance.

Fabric A
- Cut 1 piece 21½″ × 25½″ for the center panel.
- Cut 4 strips 7½″ × the fabric width for the outer border.

Fabric B
- Cut 2 strips 1½″ × 25½″ for the inner border.
- Cut 2 strips 1½″ × 23½″ for the inner border.

Fabric C
- Cut enough 2⅛″-wide bias strips to total 200″ for the binding. (See Cutting Bias Strips, page 14.)

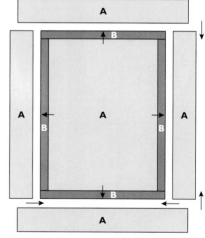 Quilt Assembly

1. Sew a 1½″ × 25½″ Fabric B inner border strip to the long opposite sides of the 21½″ × 25½″ Fabric A square. Press. Sew a 1½″ × 23½″ Fabric B inner border strip to the top and bottom of the square. Press.

2. Refer to Butted Borders on page 10. Measure the quilt top through the center from top to bottom. Trim two 7½″-wide Fabric A outer border strips to this measurement. Sew a trimmed border strip to opposite sides of the quilt. Press.

3. Measure the quilt top through the center from side to side, including the borders just added. Trim the remaining 7½″-wide outer border strips to this measurement. Sew a trimmed border strip to the top and bottom of the quilt. Press.

Assembly diagram

4. Divide one side of the quilt top into equal segments and mark the divisions. Fold the opposite edge up to the marked side and repeat the markings. Do the same for the other sides.

5. Decide how deep you want the scallops to be and make registration marks on the border. Trace a plate or something similar to mark the scallops.

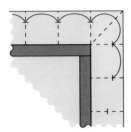

 Finishing

1. Follow the general instructions on pages 11–14 to layer, baste, and quilt your quilt. Keep the quilting designs within the marked scallops on the border.

An example of a quilting design

tip This is a great project for practicing your machine quilting.

2. Sew the 2⅛″-wide Fabric C strips together end to end with diagonal seams to make 200″ of bias binding. Press.

3. Machine baste a scant ¼″ inside the marked scallop. Trim the layers along the marked scallop line.

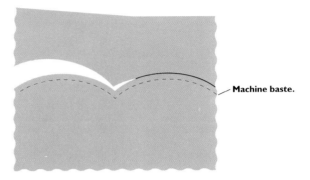

Machine baste.

4. Make a mark ¼″ inside each dent. Clip the raw edge at each dent, stopping just before the mark and basting stitches.

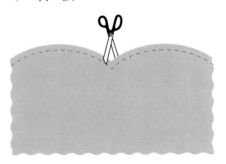

5. Working from the front, begin pinning the binding to the quilt, aligning the raw edge of the binding with the raw edge of the quilt top. Start on the side of a scallop rather than at the center of a scallop or in a dent. Place the pins perpendicular to the edge of the quilt. Do not stretch the binding; ease it gently around the curve.

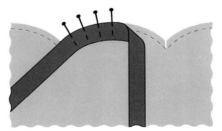

6. When you reach the first dent, *gently* spread the scallop to create a straight line. Continue pinning the binding on this "straight edge," placing a pin on either side of the dent to keep the binding aligned. Continue pinning the binding all around the quilt edges.

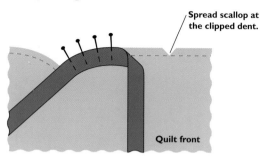

Spread the scallop at the dent.

7. Working from the back, stitch the binding to the quilt with a ¼″ seam. Remove each pin as you reach it. Stitch each dent just as you pinned it—by gently separating the scallop to sew a straight line. Make sure to stay on the inside of the clip. Join the ends of the binding as described in Binding, Steps 9 and 10, on page 14.

8. Beginning along one side of a scallop, turn the binding over the raw edge of the quilt and use matching-colored thread and an invisible stitch to secure the binding to the quilt back. Work one scallop at a time; stop just before you reach each dent.

9. At a dent, make a small fold in the binding and carefully coax the fold to the back of the quilt. Cover the seamline with the binding, match the fold to the point of the dent, and continue stitching. Repeat until the entire binding is secured.

Match the fold to the point of the dent.

baby blessings

Baby Blessings *Pieced and machine tacked by Alex Anderson, 2004.*

Quilt top size: 39½″ × 40½″

Finished block size: 6½″

Number of blocks: 15 (13 pieced, 2 plain)

Skill level: A bit more challenging, but you can do it!

When I first heard about Minkee Blankee, a cuddly new fabric being introduced to quilters, I knew I had to try it in one of the quilts for this book. Minkee Blankee is 100% polyester, doesn't shrink, and comes in a wide variety of colors (including some yummy pastels) and two plush finishes—matte (smooth) and raised dot. While it can sometimes have a mind of its own, you can control it easily with wider-than-usual seam allowances and lots of pins. Believe me, the results are definitely worth it! In *Baby Blessings*, I paired Minkee with cottons, but you can use flannels for an even softer quilt. If your local shop doesn't carry Minkee, be sure to ask about it.

 ## Materials

Minkee Blankee is 58/60″ wide. All other fabric amounts are based on a 42″ fabric width.

Alphabet-print yardage, alphabet panels, or other cotton theme fabric suitable for fussy cutting (Fabric A): ⅝ yard for blocks*

Assorted polka-dot and striped cotton prints and Minkee Blankee fabrics (matte and raised dot) in 3 or 4 coordinating pastel colors (Fabric B): ¼ yard each of approximately 12 fabrics for blocks and sashing

White Minkee Blankee (matte) (Fabric C): ¼ yard for plain blocks

White Minkee Blankee (raised dot) (Fabric D): ¾ yard for sashing and border

Pastel blue-and-white polka-dot cotton fabric (Fabric E): 1½ yards for ruffle

Backing: 1¼ yards of fabric**

* Yardage will vary depending upon the size and repeat of the print you select.

** I used white Minkee Blankee matte.

 ## Cutting

All measurements include a ½″-wide seam allowance.

Fabric A
■ Cut a total of 13 squares or rectangles for blocks. These can vary in size, ranging from 3½″ to 5½″ on a side (e.g., 3½″ × 3½″; 4¼″ × 5″).

Fabric B
■ Cut 1 strip 4½″ × the fabric width from *each* fabric for blocks.

Fabric C
■ Cut 2 squares 7½″ × 7½″ for plain blocks.

Fabric D
■ Cut 1 strip 4½″ × the fabric width for sashing.
■ Cut 4 strips 4″ × the fabric width for border.

Fabric E
■ Cut 9 strips 5″ × the fabric width for ruffle.

Making the Blocks

Remember to use a ½"-wide seam allowance.

1. Sew a 4½"-wide Fabric B strip to one side of a Fabric A rectangle or square. Trim as shown.

2. Sew a matching-colored 4½"-wide Fabric B strip to each remaining side of the unit from Step 1.

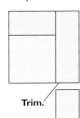

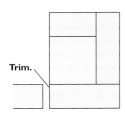

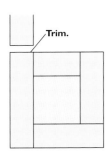

3. Use a square ruler to trim the block to 7½" × 7½", tilting the ruler to achieve a "wonky" look.

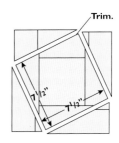

4. Repeat Steps 1–3 to make 13 blocks. Vary the angle of the square ruler when trimming the blocks to give each a unique look.

Quilt Assembly

Remember to use a ½"-wide seam allowance.

1. Cut the leftover 4½"-wide Fabric B strips and the 4½"-wide Fabric D strip into segments, varying in length from 3½" to 7½". Sew these assorted segments together randomly end to end, with straight seams, trimming as necessary, to make a 33½"-long pieced sashing strip. Make 4.

2. Arrange the pieced blocks, the 7½" Fabric C blocks, and the pieced sashing strips in 7 horizontal rows, alternating them as shown in the assembly diagram. Sew the pieced blocks and Fabric C blocks together into rows. Sew the rows of blocks and sashing strips together.

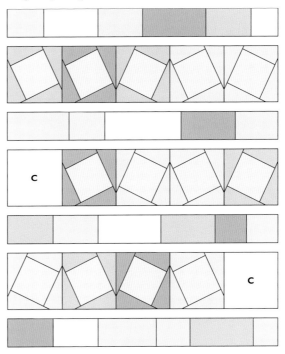

Assembly diagram

3. Refer to Butted Borders on page 10. Measure the quilt top through the center from top to bottom. Trim two 4˝-wide Fabric D border strips to this measurement. Sew a trimmed border strip to opposite sides of the quilt.

4. Measure the quilt top through the center from side to side, including the borders just added. Trim the remaining 4˝-wide border strips to this measurement. Sew a trimmed border strip to the top and bottom of the quilt.

Finishing

1. To make the ruffle, piece the 5˝-wide Fabric E strips together end to end with diagonal seams. Press the pieced strip in half lengthwise, wrong sides together. To hem the ends, fold both short raw edges under ¼˝, and then ¼˝ again. Press. Stitch the hems in place with matching-colored thread.

> *tip* If you prefer, you can substitute pom-poms, rickrack, braid, or other favorite "funky" decorative trim for the ruffle on your Minkee quilt. Just be sure it is attached securely and will not provide a choking hazard for baby!

2. Use your sewing machine to stitch a gathering stitch along the long raw edge of the strip with a ¼˝-wide seam allowance. (I used a wide zigzag stitch over perle cotton, as shown below.) Gather the ruffle to measure approximately 160˝.

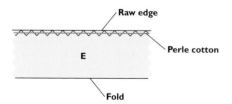

Raw edge

Perle cotton

E

Fold

3. Pin the ruffle to the front side of the quilt top, aligning the raw edges. Adjust the gathers as necessary and overlap the finished ends slightly. Machine baste the ruffle to the quilt with a large basting stitch using a ⅜˝ seam allowance.

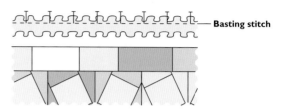

Basting stitch

> *tip* I folded the long ruffle into quarters and placed marker pins to help me evenly distribute the ruffle around the quilt's perimeter.

4. To make the backing, measure the quilt top and cut a piece of the backing fabric to the top's dimensions.

5. Layer the backing and quilt top right sides together. The basted ruffle will be sandwiched inside, between the quilt top and the backing. Sew around the perimeter of the quilt top with a ½˝-wide seam allowance, leaving an 8˝ opening for turning. Trim any excess backing even with the quilt top and clip the corners. Turn the quilt right side out. With matching-colored thread, hand stitch the opening closed. Sew from the back, using a blind stitch.

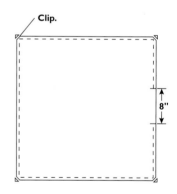

Clip.

8"

> *tip* Since there is no batting in this quilt, no quilting is necessary. I machine tacked at various intersections to secure the layers.

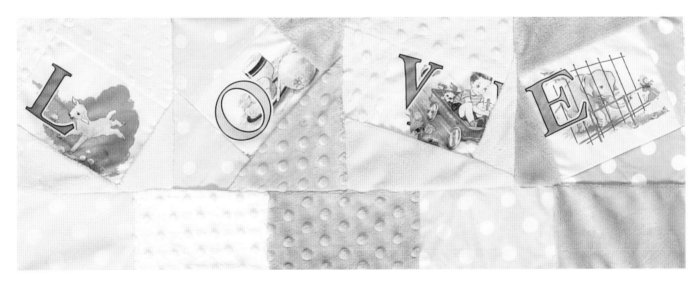

grandma's
favorite

Grandma's Favorite *Pieced by Alex Anderson, 2004. Machine quilted by Paula Reid.*

Quilt top size: 41¼" × 45½"

Finished block size: 3"

Number of blocks: 32

Skill level: A bit more challenging, but you can do it!

With its gentle palette of neutral-colored prints, *Grandma's Favorite* makes an excellent choice for a christening quilt. You can duplicate my single-color scheme; select another favorite color, such as the primary color in the nursery décor; or enjoy mixing a variety of colors (pastels would be perfect!) in this "heirloom" strippy-style design.

tip You may wish to cut a few extra 1½" squares to give you even more flexibility in your fabric choices as you construct the blocks.

Materials

Fabric amounts are based on a 42" fabric width.

Assorted white-on-white, cream, and beige prints (Fabric A): 1½ yards total for blocks, setting triangles, and binding*

Cream swirly print (Fabric B): 1⅓ yards for sashing strips and outer border

Medium beige print (Fabric C): ¼ yard for inner border

Backing: 2½ yards of fabric

Batting: 45" × 49" piece

I used approximately 20 different prints.

Cutting

All measurements include a ¼"-wide seam allowance.

Fabric A
- Cut a total of 288 squares 1½" × 1½" in matching sets of 4 and 5 for the blocks.
- Cut a total of 14 squares 5½" × 5½"; then cut each square in half twice diagonally to make 4 triangles (56 total) for the side setting triangles.*
- Cut a total of 8 squares 3" × 3"; then cut each square in half once diagonally to make 2 triangles (16 total) for the corner setting triangles.
- Cut a total of 5 strips 2⅛" × the fabric width for the binding.

Fabric B
- Cut 3 strips, from the lengthwise grain, 4¾" × 34½" for the sashing strips.
- Cut 4 strips, from the lengthwise grain, 5" × the fabric length for the outer border.

Fabric C
- Cut 4 strips 1½" × the fabric width for the inner border.

I cut these from cream and beige fabrics.

 Making the Blocks

1. Arrange nine 1½" × 1½" Fabric A squares (5 of one fabric and 4 of another contrasting fabric) in one of the configurations shown here and in the quilt photo.

Use contrasting Fabric A squares.

2. Sew the squares into rows. Press. Sew the rows together. Press. Make 32 total, some in each desired configuration.

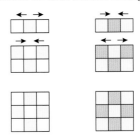

Make 32 total.

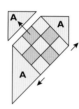 # Quilt Assembly

1. Arrange the blocks on point in 4 vertical rows of 8 blocks each as shown in the assembly diagram on. Add the Fabric A side and corner setting triangles.

2. Working with the first vertical row, stitch the blocks, side triangles, and corner triangles together in diagonal sections, as shown.

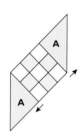

Top diagonal section

Center sections

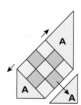

Bottom diagonal section

3. Sew together the diagonal sections from Step 2, as shown in the assembly diagram. Repeat Steps 2 and 3 for the remaining 3 vertical rows.

Assembly diagram

4. Arrange the pieced rows from Step 3 and the 4¾"-wide Fabric B sashing strips side by side, alternating them as shown in the assembly diagram. Sew the pieced rows and sashing strips together. Press.

5. Refer to Butted Borders on page 10. Measure the quilt top through the center from top to bottom. Trim each 1½"-wide Fabric C inner border strip to this measurement. Sew a trimmed border strip to opposite sides of the quilt. Press.

6. Measure the quilt top through the center from side to side, including the borders just added. Trim the remaining 1½"-wide inner border strips to this measurement. Sew a trimmed border strip to the top and bottom of the quilt. Press.

7. Repeat Steps 5 and 6 to trim and sew a 5"-wide Fabric B outer border strip to the sides, top, and bottom of the quilt. Press.

Finishing

Follow the general instructions on pages 11–14 to layer, baste, and quilt your quilt. Sew the 2⅛"-wide Fabric A strips together end to end with diagonal seams and use them to bind the edges. For this quilt, I used an assortment of the Fabric A prints for the binding.

about the author

Alex Anderson's love affair with quilt-making began in 1978, when she completed her *Grandmother's Flower Garden* quilt as part of her work toward a degree in art at San Francisco State University. Over the years, her focus has rested on understanding fabric relationships and on an intense appreciation for traditional quilting surface design and star quilts.

Alex currently hosts the popular Home and Garden Television and DIY Network quilt show *Simply Quilts* and is a spokesperson for Bernina of America. Her quilts have appeared in numerous magazines, often in articles devoted specifically to her work.

Alex has two children and lives in Northern California with her husband, their dog, and the challenges of feeding various forms of wildlife in her backyard. Visit her website at alexandersonquilts.com.

Other Books by Alex Anderson

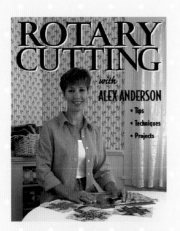

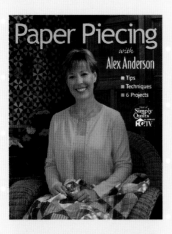

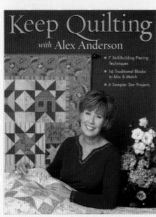

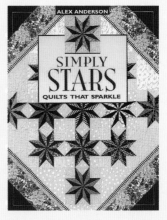

Great Titles
from C&T PUBLISHING